HANNAH
AND HECTOR

LOVE
COLLECTORS

B. JANE TURNQUEST
Illustrated by Vasilisa Erisova

B. Jane Turnquest is a writer of books for children and adults; she also pens songs for her personal cathartic ministry. She lives in The Bahamas - to find out more about what she is writing, follow her on Facebook at B.Jane Turnquest Children's Book and Facebook & Instagram at Quill Ink Parchment Publish.

Children's books by B. Jane Turnquest

The Memoir That Makes You Go Mmm

Pompa Pumpity

The Stepmother, Little Grace and The Fig Tree

The Contrite Contrary Chronicles

Sir Caerwyn The Knight and the Midnight Colored Plight

Caerwyn and The Heart of The Sea

The Loot On Cute : Papers on Proprieties

Amount To What Counts : Papers on Proprieties

Facts Acts Youth Enrichment on Tact : Papers on Proprieties

Quest To be Your Best : Papers on Proprieties

The Legend of The Mean Mother

If You Ever Meet A Bahamian Mermaid

Book Of Knowledge Journal

Franc (Oh!) Phile

Tickled Thinglish

Tickled Blinglish

Mermaids' Birthday Love & Wishes

Our books may be purchased in bulk for promotional, educational, or business use. Please contact your local bookseller
or Quill Ink & Parchment Publication at email info@quillinkparchment.com

Quill Ink & Parchment

P U B L I C A T I O N S

23 Rhuidrock Towers, Nassau, Bahamas SP 60276

www.quillinkparchment.com

For Jude
and Karter

Hannah and Hector were
two fine twins.
They were sharing a message;
that love is where
happiness begins.

This was Hannah and Hector's
mission to spread.
They painted the world
with happiness, smiles and
their favorite color, red.

HERE IS HANNAH AND HECTOR'S CREED.

Guess what a hero needs?
It is not strength, invisibility
or speed.
Here is another clue
for you.
To be a hero, change one
letter in 'cape.'
Then add an 'r' in its place,
and a new ability will
take shape.

The twins' superpower was in their hearts and minds. It was all about a choice, and the action behind it, which was simple;

BE KIND!

How did Hannah and Hector

go about this?

What was the method they

used, their basis?

It was not a secret,

so be sure not to keep it!

With lots of heart
was how their works were done and how each move
and mission would start.
They applied what they called action–driven–givings.
This was sprinkled with free, small, thoughtful acts that
they thought would enrich someone's living.

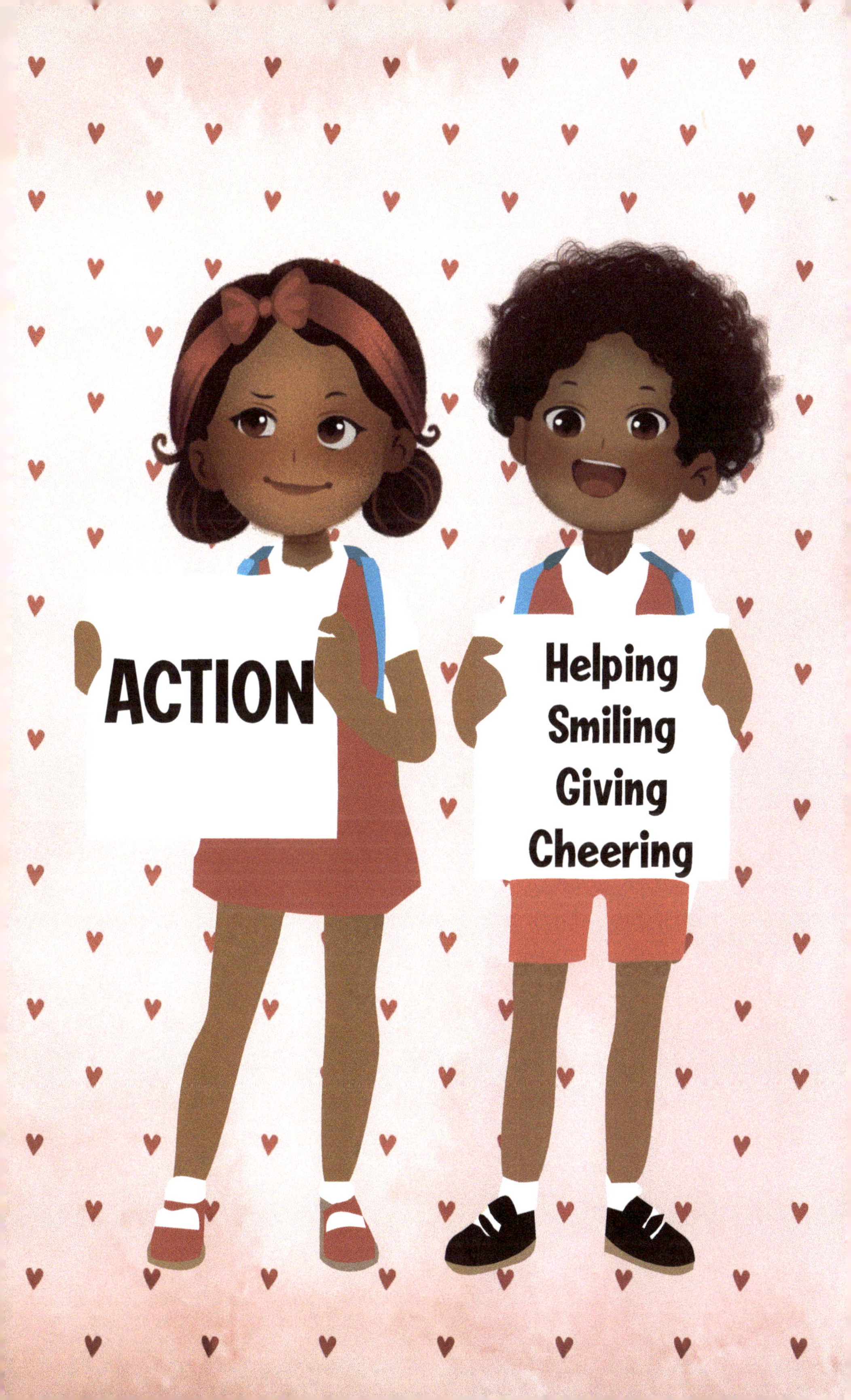
ACTION
Helping
Smiling
Giving
Cheering

Are you wondering how love looks
and how it feels?
It looks like a smile, a hug and a
helping hand. It feels warm and
special – and for the person who
gets it, it feels like a huge deal!

To tell it plainly, it is a
selfless gift,
that is so mighty, it can,
without fail, uplift.

Here are a few of Hannah and
Hector's top missions.
Study the examples, learn
and listen.
Try some out, or hunt for other
goodness to create;
if you are brave, if you dare
to be someone who can
make the world a little bit
better, or even great.

According to the twins,
LOVE looks like a win!

This is Hannah and Hector's

Love Collection **TOP TEN**.

Just so you know, their list

is ongoing; it has no end.

...and what do they gain,

what is it exactly that

they collect?

They get things such as

gratitude, a friend and of

course, smiles –

positive effects.

If you see a teacher with a load,

go into **volunteer** mode.

Consider what an **animal**

may be needing;

petting, giving water and,

if necessary, feeding.

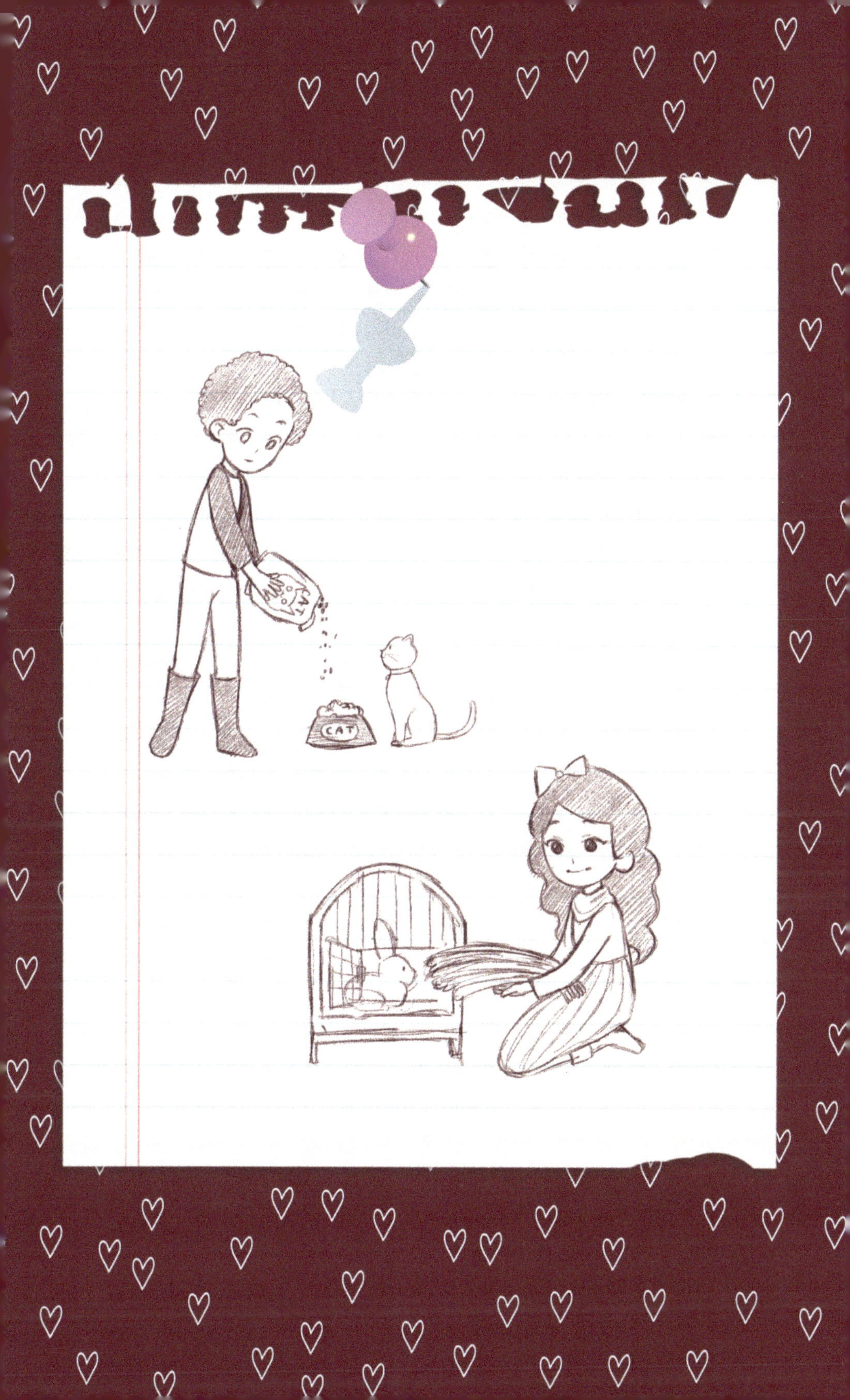
CAT

3

Telling someone hi leaves them feeling seen and less shy.

Flip a coin for an **orphan** or **widow**.

Where it lands is where your time

or token of giving is to go.

widow

orphan

Search for the most **unpopular kid** in school.

Here is something you can do that would be

super, extremely and unforgettably cool.

Find out their birthday.

On that day, hang a bright banner greeting,

announcing it, put it where all could see the

special display.

Practice love and kindness with

your family and friends.

Be dependable, be their biggest fan

— but when something goes wrong,

work together to make amends.

Show others that they have **equal** value,

no matter their grades, abilities, size,

shape, any other differences or hue.

The **truth** is always kind. So when

someone is on a path that is wrong,

tell them that is not a good place,

and not where they belong.

The easiest on this list to do is
give a **compliment**.

Find something genuine and good about

someone – there is never a need to invent.

If you cannot think of anything pleasant

and kind to say,

simply think harder and positively,

and it will come your way.

Uplift or lend a hand
when someone falls or cannot stand.
When someone fails or flops,
encourage them to go at it again
and not give up or stop.

This is another secret you must not keep!
Tell or show others; that sometimes you win,
and sometimes you have defeats.
And that it is life, and it's okay
because next time for a win
could simply be another day.

Acts like these are what

Hannah and Hector do.

They hope that now that

you have read this,

you would sprinkle and

collect some love too.

We hope
you enjoyed!

Show the author
some LOVE and
ask your parent
to leave a review
on Amazon!

Shake-a-Tail WEATHER

Sunkanoo, The Mermaids' Big Splash

B. Jane Turnquest
Vasilisa Erisova

tickled BLINGLISH

Add glitz to what you say with spectacular adjectives!

what happens when your words are ultra ~~bedazzling?~~ frazzling!!

B. Jane Turnquest
Illustrated by Vasilisa Erisova

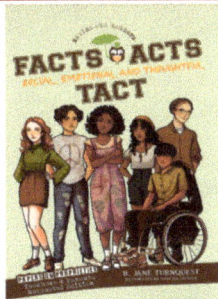
FACTS & ACTS TACT
Social, Emotional, and Theatrical Tact
B. Jane Turnquest

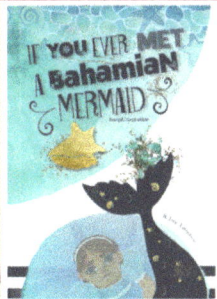
IF YOU EVER MET A Bahamian MERMAID

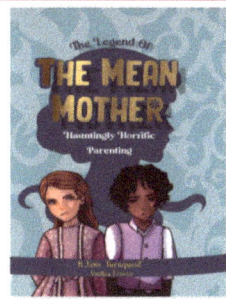
The Legend Of THE MEAN MOTHER
'Hauntingly 'Horrific' Parenting
B. Jane Turnquest

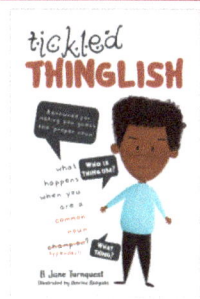
tickled THINGLISH

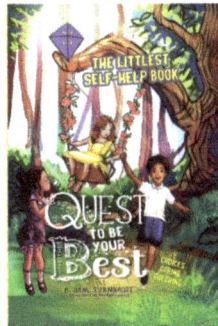
THE LITTLEST SELF-HELP BOOK
QUEST TO BE YOUR Best
B. Jane Turnquest

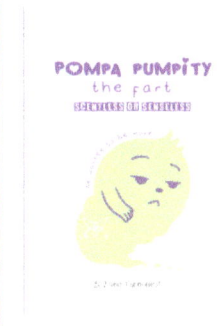
POMPA PUMPITY the Fart
SCENTLESS OR SCENDLESS

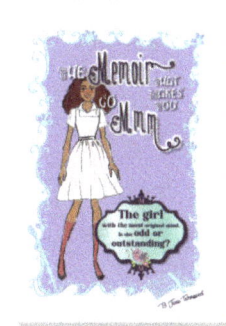
The Memoir that makes you Go Mum
The girl with the most original about is she odd or outstanding?
B. Jane Turnquest

THE STEPMOTHER, LITTLE GRACE & THE FIG TREE

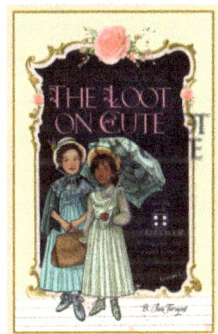
THE LOOT ON CUTE

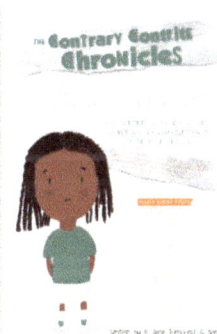
The Contrary Contrix Chronicles
Written by B. Jane Turnquest & Son
Illustrated by

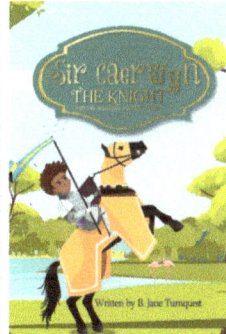
Sir Caerwyn THE KNIGHT
Written by B. Jane Turnquest

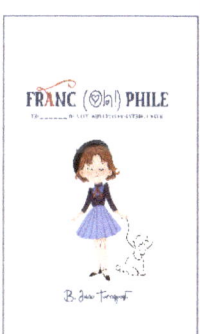
FRANC (Oh) PHILE
B. Jane Turnquest

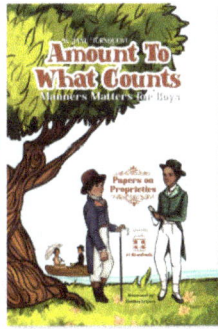
Amount To What Counts
Manners Matters for Boys

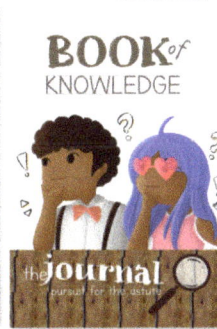
BOOK of KNOWLEDGE
the JOURNAL
pursuit for the astute

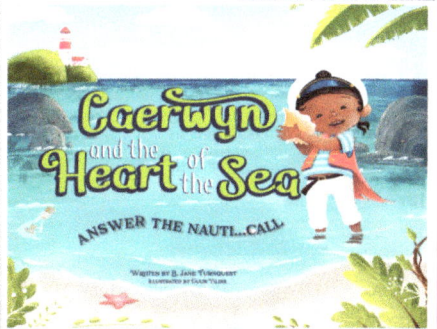
Caerwyn and the Heart of the Sea
ANSWER THE NAUTI...CALL
Written by B. Jane Turnquest
Illustrated by

www.ingramcontent.com/pod-product-compliance
Lightning Source LLC
Chambersburg PA
CBHW040827300326
41914CB00058B/1236